A World of Difference

Shake, Rattle, and Strum

By Sara Corbett

CHILDRENS PRESS®
CHICAGO

Picture Acknowledgements

Cover (top left), NASA; cover (left), © Gary Conner/PhotoEdit; cover (top right, bottom right), 1, © Lee Boltin; 3 left, © Bill Aron/PhotoEdit; 3 (right), © Robert Frerck/Odyssey/Frerck/Chicago; 4 (left), © Robert E. Daemmrich/Tony Stone Images; 4 (right), © Victor Englebert; 5 (left), © Robert Frerck/Odyssey/Frerck/Chicago; 5 (top right), © Murray & Associates/Tony Stone Images; 5 (bottom right), © Jack Vartoogian; 6 (left), Bishop Museum, The State Museum of Natural and Cultural History; 6 (right), © Lee Boltin; 7 (left), © Victor Englebert; 7 (top right), © Jacques Jangoux/Tony Stone Images; 7 (bottom right), © J. Nettis/H. Armstrong Roberts; 8 (left), © Brian Seed/Tony Stone Images; 8 (top right), © Donna Carroll/Travel Stock; 8 (bottom right), © Reinhard Brucker; 9 (left), © Cameramann International, Ltd.; 9 (right), © Robert Frerck/Odyssey/Frerck/ Chicago; 10 (left), © Kurt Scholz/SuperStock International, Inc.; 10 (top right), © John Elk/Tony Stone Images; 10 (bottom right), © Jack Vartoogian; 11 (left), 11 (right), © Lee Boltin; 12 (left) © Cameramann International, Ltd.; 12 (right), © Tony Morrison; 13 (top right), © Jack Vartoogian; 13 (bottom left), © Reinhard Brucker; 13 (bottom right), © John LaDue/Root Resources; 14 (left), Bob and Ira Spring; 14 (right), © Robert Frerck/Tony Stone Images; 15 (top left), © Porterfield/Chickering; 15 (bottom left), © Reinhard Brucker/Field Museum, Chicago; 15 (top right), © Donna Carroll/Travel Stock; 15 (bottom right), © Hal Linker/ SuperStock International, Inc.; 16 (left), © Frank Siteman/Tony Stone Images; 6 (top right), 16 (bottom right), © Cameramann International, Ltd.; 17 (top), © Geisser/H. Armstrong Roberts; 17 (bottom), © Steve Vidler/SuperStock International, Inc.; 18 (left), The Shrine to Music Museum University of South Dakota; 18 (top right), © The Field Museum of Natural History Neg #A111207©, Chicago; 18 (bottom right), © Suzanne Murphy/Tony Stone Images; 19 (top right), © Wendy Stone/Odyssey/ Chicago; 20 (left), © Jason Laure; 20 (right), Photri; 21 (bottom left), © Victor Englebert; 21 (top right), © Robert Frerck/ Odyssey/Frerck/Chicago; 21 (bottom right), © Bill Aron/PhotoEdit; 22 (left), Stock Montage; 22 (right), © David Shores/Unicorn Stock Photos; 23 (top left), © Lee Boltin; 23 (bottom), The Shrine to Music Museum University of South Dakota; 23 (top right), © Cameramann International, Ltd.; 24 (left), © J.Eastcott/Y.Momatiuk/Valan; 24 (top right), © Erwin C. Bud Nielsen; 24 (bottom right), © Cameramann International, Ltd.; 25 (top), © C. Bucks/H. Armstrong Roberts; 25 (bottom), © Phil Borden/PhotoEdit; 26 (left), The Bettmann Archive; 26 (right), © Lee Boltin; 27 (left), The Shrine to Music Museum University of South Dakota; 27 (right), The Bettmann Archive; 28 (left), © Aneal Vohra/Unicorn Stock Photos; 28 (top right), The Shrine to Music Museum University of South Dakota; 28 (bottom right), © H. Abernathy/H. Armstrong Roberts; 29 (top left), © Tony Morrison; 29 (top right), © Aneal Vohra/Unicorn Stock Photos; 29 (bottom), © Buddy Mays/Travel Stock; 30 (left), © Cameramann International, Ltd.; 30 (top right), © Porterfield/Chickering; 30 (bottom right), © Lee Boltin; 31 (top left), © Robert Frerck/Odyssey/Chicago; 31 (top right), © Virginia R. Grimes; 31 (bottom right), © Victor Englebert

On the cover	On the title page
Top: 6th-century Mexican ceramic double flute	19th-century English serpent horn
Bottom left: Korean drum	
Bottom right: 15th-century English gitern	

Project Editor Shari Joffe
Design Herman Adler Design Group
Photo Research Feldman & Associates

Corbett, Sara.
    Shake, rattle, and strum / by Sara Corbett.
        p. cm. — (A world of difference)
    Includes index.
    ISBN 0-516-08194-2
    1. Musical instruments — Juvenile literature. 2. Musical instruments —
Pictorial works — Juvenile literature. [1. Musical instruments.]
I. Title. II. Series.
ML 460.C72 1995
784.19 — dc20   94-36343
                                                                      CIP
                                                                    AC MN

Contents

Starting Off On a Good Note **4**

What is a Musical Instrument, Anyway? **8**

Musical Families **10**

Making Music from Scratch **12**

Musical Moods **16**

Magical Instruments **18**

Keeping the Beat **20**

You Are What You Play **22**

Whistle While You Work **24**

Hearing It Through the Grapevine **26**

Musical Migration **28**

Staying Tuned to Tradition **30**

Glossary **32**

Index **32**

Starting Off On a Good Note

Do you play a musical instrument? If you do, have you ever thought about the reasons why?

Maybe it's because you want to join a band or orchestra. Maybe playing a certain instrument is a tradition in your family or your culture. Maybe your parents are making you take lessons! Perhaps you admire someone who plays your kind of instrument, or maybe you want to be a professional musician someday. More than anything, you probably play an instrument because it's fun to do!

If you think you've never played a musical instrument, stop and think again: have you ever blown a whistle or rung a bell? Have you played a kazoo? These, too, are musical instruments!

Griots, Niger In western Africa, traveling musicians are called *griots*. Tribal histories are often told through their performances.

Young trumpet player, United States

Classical musicians, India Indian classical music often consists of two or three players who improvise on set musical patterns called *talas* and *ragas.*

Musical instruments have many uses, actually. Everybody knows that music can be entertaining. But instruments can do more than please an audience. Around the world, they play a big role in religion, celebration, communication, and even politics and war. In fact, you can travel anywhere on earth and you'll find musical instruments in almost every culture along the way.

***Gamelan* orchestra, Bali, Indonesia** A *gamelan,* an Indonesian type of orchestra, includes xylophones, gongs, and other percussion instruments. *Gamelans* often perform at religious and political ceremonies— and sometimes at puppet shows!

Japanese *gagaku* ensemble *Gagaku* is the traditional music of Japan. The melody is played by horns, flutes, and string instruments. Bronze gongs of various sizes are hit to emphasize the beat of the music.

But is a musical instrument in Polynesia going to look like one from South America? Is it going to look like an instrument from your school band? No way, right?

In Polynesia, you'll find native groups playing the *fango-fango,* or nose flute. (That's right, they play them with their noses!) A popular instrument in South Africa is the *ombgwe,* which looks a little like an oversized lollipop. It is made from a stick of cane and the hollow fruit of the *nsala.* And in the Andes Mountains of Bolivia, the Quechua people play bamboo pipes that are held to the side.

Mexican ceramic double flute, c. 550 A.D.

These instruments are as different from each other as the cultures they come from. Polynesia, South Africa, and Bolivia are thousands of miles apart. They have different climates, social customs, resources, languages—and different kinds of music that are considered beautiful. All these differences are reflected in the musical instruments played in each of the cultures.

At the same time, the *fango-fango,* the *ombgwe,* and the Quechua bamboo instrument are each a type of flute. They work the same way the flute in your school band does: with sound created from air that is blown across a hollow tube with holes in it to vary the note. Imagine that! Even with all the miles between us and these other cultures, our musical instruments can have a lot in common!

Nasal notes The nose flute, or *fango-fango,* has special significance in the South Pacific, since many of the island cultures believe that the air that comes from your nose carries the soul. Islanders play the flute with one nostril, usually blocking the other with their thumb.

Quechua Indians playing side-blown flutes, Bolivia A side-blown flute is a pipe with the blow hole pierced in its side. It is usually held to the right of the player.

Samburu man playing end-blown flute, Kenya End-blown flutes are usually somewhat long and have only three or four finger holes.

Modern orchestral flute The Western classical flute, a side-blown flute, reached Europe from Asia in the 1200s. For many years, it was made from wood and had no keys on it, so it looked a lot like the flutes found in China, Africa, and Polynesia. Today, orchestral flutes are made of silver or brass and have 21 keys, giving them a wide range of musical notes.

What is a Musical Instrument, Anyway?

Do you sometimes tap a pencil to the rhythm of your favorite song? Does this mean your pencil counts as a musical instrument? That's a tough question to answer. It would be easy to say that only things that are built to produce music can be musical instruments. But in fact, many instruments were discovered quite by accident!

For instance, some scientists believe that thousands of years ago, a prehistoric hunter discovered that if he plucked his hunting bow, it would make an interesting sound. This was the beginning of a long history of stringed instruments. The musical bow, which is modeled

Conch shell, Tahiti The conch shell horn, an ancient type of instrument, was probably discovered after a satisfying meal of conch meat!

Hopi wooden scraper, southwestern United States
A scraper is a notched instrument that makes a rasping sound when rubbed by a stick or a piece of bone. Scrapers have been around for thousands of years.

Xhosha woman playing mouth bow, South Africa
Musical bows are the oldest and simplest of string instruments. Different forms of the musical bow are found all over the globe, from Africa and Asia to the Americas. Often, a hollow object called a *resonator* is used to amplify a string instrument's sound. This might be a gourd, a tin can, or, as in this case, the player's mouth!

Fijian stamping sticks In Fiji, two hollow bamboo sticks are pounded on the ground to the rhythm of the music.

Zuni gourd rattle Many rattles were discovered by shaking natural objects, like seed pods, dried fruits, and gourds. Gourds are easy to carry and are found all over the world, making them very common materials for musical instruments. The Zuni people of New Mexico use rattles in their ceremonial dances.

after the hunting bow and is one of the oldest known musical instruments, could probably be considered the great, great, great grandparent of the harp!

Other instruments that have been around a long time are different kinds of clappers, scrapers, and rattles, most of which were discovered by people as they went through their daily routines of gathering food and taking care of their homes. In Bali, for example, the use of stamping sticks as a musical instrument came about as villagers did their daily chore of grinding corn in a trough. The regular rhythm of the sticks helped make the work go faster.

Musical Families

When looking at musical instruments around the world, you'll discover that similar kinds of instruments pop up in different cultures—even among cultures that have never had any contact with each other! For instance, versions of the trumpet are played from Mongolia to Mexico, and nearly everywhere in between. This is because even though

Scottish bagpipes (wind family) Wind instruments are sounded by the player's breath. The air may be blown across a hole in the instrument, or into the instrument through a mouthpiece or vibrating reed.

Ghanaian drums (percussion family) Percussion instruments are those that are struck or shaken to produce sound.

Chinese "moon guitar" (string family) With string instruments, sound is produced when a stretched string is vibrated by being bowed or plucked.

18th-century French harpsichord (keyboard family)
With keyboard instruments, sound is produced when the player presses keys attached to devices that either vibrate strings or blow air through pipes.

instruments come in all sorts of crazy shapes and sizes, there are a limited number of ways to produce musical sound. Most instruments fall into one of five categories: strings, winds, percussion, keyboard, or horns. These musical "families" are based on *how* the sound of the instrument is produced. Usually, you can identify an instrument's family just by looking at the instrument. Can you name an instrument from each group?

Making Music from Scratch

If you wanted a musical instrument today, where would you get it? You'd probably go to a music store and buy one, right? Well, in many parts of the world, it would be very difficult to find a store, let alone one that sells instruments. Can you imagine a music store in the Saharan desert or the Alaskan tundra? What about in a mountaintop village in Tibet? Even in this country, music stores are a relatively recent addition to society. This means that people have had to learn how to build musical instruments from materials available in their own environment.

Traditional *charango*, Bolivia
This small, sturdy guitar was made from the horny skin of the armadillo, an animal common to South America. The armadillo is now protected by law, so modern *charangos* are made from wood.

From log to finished drum
In Papua New Guinea, where most of the land is covered with thick, tropical forests, wood is a common drum material.

Egyptian folk singers playing *rebabs* The *rebab* is a two-stringed Arab fiddle. Its resonator, or soundbox, is often made from a coconut shell!

African long drum with snakeskin head, Cameroon

Sheepskin bagpipe, Czech Republic Bagpipes made of animal skin are found in Europe, Asia, and North Africa.

Scientists who study the similarities and differences between cultures are called anthropologists. For an anthropologist, musical materials provide exciting clues. By looking at what an instrument is made of, you can often deduce some specific information about the culture that it comes from. For example, the Apache, a Native American group, make a fiddle from a hollowed-out cactus. This helps us to assume that the Apache live in a hot, dry climate, like that found in the southwestern United States.

Bamboo trumpet, Sulawesi, Indonesia Instruments made of bamboo are common in warm, tropical countries like Indonesia, where bamboo plants grow plentifully.

Gourd xylophone, Guatemala Xylophones with gourd resonators can be found in Latin America and Africa.

Caribbean steel-drum band The steel drum is popularly considered the national instrument of Trinidad. It was invented in the 1940s when local people discovered empty oil drums, left on the beach by American military forces during World War II. Talk about recycling!

Musical saw player, Denmark Even a plain old saw can be turned into a musical instrument!

Iroquois turtle-shell rattle, North America In many cultures, rattles made from plants or animals are used for ceremonial purposes.

Let the termites do the work A favorite instrument of the Australian Aborigines is the *didgeridoo*. First, a long eucalyptus branch is buried in the ground. Termites then eat away at the soft wood until what's left is a perfectly hollowed-out horn! The Aborigines then dig it up, paint it, and play it.

Musical Moods

Samisen player, Japan
Tea ceremonies are formal events in Japan. Musicians often play the *samisen,* a long-necked lute, and the *biwa,* a short-necked lute, to maintain the appropriate peaceful mood.

When you're feeling happy, do you listen to a certain kind of music? What about when you're sad or angry? This is one of the great things about musical instruments; they help both the musician and the listener express certain feelings. Music can have a big influence on your mood. Among the Akan people of Ghana, there is a flute player who follows the king around day and night, playing music to control his moods. When there is a crisis, it's important that the flute player choose the right music to keep the king calm. Wouldn't it be fun to have music with you wherever you go?

Somber sounds
In Russia, bells are sometimes rung during memorial services to honor the dead.

Jaw harp The jaw harp makes a sort of twang when it's played. Because it can echo loudly through the valleys in the European Alps, even today Austrian boys play the jaw harp to express love to their sweethearts.

Local festival, Switzerland
Often, you'll find festive music at the heart of a cultural celebration or social event.

Musical instruments can express everything from sorrow to joy to rebellion. You will often find musical instruments at the heart of a celebration or social event. Back before we had stereos or radios, people used to gather around the piano for jolly sing-alongs!

Castanets Spanish *flamenca* dancers use castanets, a kind of wooden clapper, to help make their dancing faster and more spirited.

Magical Instruments

Many cultures believe that music comes from the soul, or even from the spirit world. In other words, music is thought to be magical. For this reason, musical instruments are often considered to be sacred and very powerful. In Siberia, the *nungu* is a drum with jingles attached to it, similar to a tambourine. It is played by shamans, or magical priests, who measure their magical powers by the number of jingles on their drum.

Some instruments are even believed to have power over nature.

Bull-roarers, Papua New Guinea
A bull-roarer is a flat wooden blade attached to a cord. When it is swung around quickly over the player's head, it makes a loud humming noise. In many Oceanic, African, and Native American cultures, bull-roarers are believed to have magical qualities because they are thought to express the voices of spirits, ancestors, or the forces of nature.

Dayak gong, Borneo This type of gong, used by the Dayak people of Borneo, is hung from a simple frame and struck with a padded beater. Some Borneans believe that the sound of this gong can change the course of damaging storms.

Indian snake charmer The *tiktiri* is actually a form of the clarinet, made from two cane pipes and a gourd. Snake charmers pass their art down from generation to generation. Warning: your own clarinet will not work on snakes!

Shamans with drums used in healing rituals, Zimbabwe In some cultures, healers, or shamans, use musical instruments to communicate with the spirit world.

For example, the Inuit of Alaska and northern Canada use rattles to call the salmon to shore, and in Hungary, farmers blow conch shells to make thunderstorms go away. In India, snake charmers use a type of clarinet, called the *tiktiri,* to "hypnotize" dangerous snakes.

Keeping the Beat

Another thing that demonstrates the importance of musical instruments is that they're used in so many different religious and cultural ceremonies around the world.

In China, you will find wooden drums carved to look like fish. These are called *mu-yu* ("wooden fish") or temple blocks, and are used in prayer. Because fish never seem to sleep, the shape of the *mu-yu* symbolizes prayer that never ends.

In parts of the world where two cultures come together, the result can be a curious mix of musical traditions. For example, in Africa, Ethiopian Christians will accompany their religious services with not only a church organ, but with drums and rattles, too. For the holiday of Passover, Jewish Ethiopians sing traditional Hebrew songs accompanied by gongs, drums, and a *masonquo,* an African form of the guitar.

Nfir, **Morocco** Usually five feet long, this Moroccan trumpet is made from brass and is used to signal the end of the Muslim fast of Ramadan.

Tibetan monks playing *rag-dung* trumpets
The low-pitched chanting of Tibetan Buddhist monks
is sometimes accompanied by long metal trumpets called
rag-dung. Sometimes, these trumpets are as much as
20 feet long!

Inca Sun Festival, Peru The Inca, a people who once
ruled a great South American empire, were conquered by
the Spanish in the 1500s. Descendants of the Inca have
preserved many of their traditions, such as public religious
ceremonies honoring the gods. Music and dance are
an important part of such ceremonies.

Jewish *shofar* The *shofar,* usually made from a ram's
horn, is blown on important Jewish occasions. On Rosh
Hashanah, it is sounded to welcome the religious
New Year. On Yom Kippur,
the Day of Atonement,
it is sounded as a call for
repentance and sacrifice.

**Ethiopian Orthodox
Church service** Ethiopian priests
accompany their religious ceremonies
with drums and rattles called *sistrums*.

You Are What You Play

We know that musical instruments have magical and religious power in some cultures, but what about social and political power? You bet! In fact, in parts of Africa, battles are fought over certain kinds of drums. In Ghana, the power of a tribal chief is determined by how many drums he has and how big they are. In 19th-century India, princes took a lot of pride in the various instruments in their court. They had elaborately decorated musical instruments made to demonstrate their wealth and nobility.

There's even one country whose national symbol is a musical instrument. Can you guess which one? Here's a hint: the instrument is sometimes painted green and covered with shamrocks! In some cases, an instrument indicates not only your social status, but also your gender. In some cultures, certain instruments are played only by men, while others are played only by women.

Panpipe flute, South America
In some cultures, flutes are played only by men. Among the Tucano Indians of Colombia, the number of tubes on a panpipe depends on the age of the player. Boys between the ages of five and nine have three tubes on their panpipes; full-grown men may have eight or nine.

Giraffe Piano, Czechoslovakia, 1800s In Europe in the 1700s and 1800s, it was fashionable for people to display their wealth by buying elaborate, expensive pianos.

Irish harp It's Ireland that has a musical instrument as its national symbol! Shamrock-covered harps are even found on Irish coins. Traditionally, harpists were highly respected members of Irish society. They were employed in the households of only the very wealthy and the high nobility.

Koto player, Japan The *koto*, a long zither, traditionally has been played mainly by women.

Mayuri, India The *mayuri*, a type of lute, once helped Indian princes show off the splendor of their royal courts. *Mayuri* means "peacock." Doesn't it figure that the peacock is known for its pride?

Whistle While You Work

Musical instruments sometimes help us to concentrate, or to pass time, as we work. Military bands play loud, stirring music with a strong beat so soldiers can march evenly and keep their morale up. In Switzerland, sheepherders play the *alpenhorn* to entertain themselves during the long days they spend alone. In the Congo, musicians with small, portable drums entertain brush cutters as they clear the fields for planting rice.

Musical instruments are a central part of some people's work life. In Europe, the accordian is a popular instrument among street musicians, also known as "buskers."

Street musicians, Poland

Portable pleasure Between 1914 and 1918, the musicans of Great Britain raised an enormous sum of money to buy a harmonica for every British soldier entering World War I. The harmonicas provided countless hours of entertainment for the soldiers while they were away from home.

Military band, Newfoundland

Swiss *alpenhorn* If you find yourself in Switzerland and you listen carefully, you might hear the lonely cry of the sheepherder's *alpenhorn*.

Sansa This instrument is common all over Africa. It is also known as a "thumb piano," because it is played with the thumbs and sounds a little bit like a piano. In Zaire, night watchmen often play the *sansa* to keep them awake through their watch.

In Senegal, musicians called *griots* travel from village to village, playing a type of small guitar called a *khalam* and telling stories. A griot will play at a wedding or naming ceremony in exchange for some food and a place to sleep.

Hearing it Through the Grapevine

Many cultures use different kinds of bells, whistles, horns, or drums to communicate. For example, the American military has special songs, played on a bugle, that signal the beginning and end of each day. In India, special gongs are sounded to mark the time of day.

German hunting horn Horns like this, used to sound signals during hunting trips, became popular in Europe during the Middle Ages. In the 1400s, when France began to have postal delivery service, a postman would use the same kind of horn to signal his arrival and departure in a town.

In parts of Africa, drummers "broadcast" news from village to village with special "talking" drums. These drums can actually imitate the sounds of tonal African languages, so people can listen to them the same way you might listen to news on the radio!

Military bugler, United States A bugle tells soldiers when to get up in the morning and when it's time for bed. The songs are called "Reveille" in the morning and "Taps" at the end of the day.

Kalengo talking drum, Nigeria
The *kalengo* is used almost like a telephone in parts of Nigeria. Since it makes sounds that are a lot like the local language, it can announce births, deaths, marriages, sporting events, initiation ceremonies, messages from the government, even gossip and jokes! These messages go drummer to drummer, and can be sent 100 miles or more. The pitch of the drum is changed by pressing the lacing, which alters the tightness of the drum's head.

Japanese *biwa* In ancient Japan, bards (traveling poet-singers) often played the *biwa,* a type of Japanese lute, while telling their tales of *samurai* battles and adventures.

What about you? Have you ever heard a dinner bell ring? A church bell? Or a police whistle sound in traffic? If you take a good look around, you'll find that musical instruments are an important part of communication in everyday life.

Musical Migration

Sometimes instruments can provide a sort of "musical map" of trade and travel between different cultures. For instance, if you visit Portugal, you might come across a small guitar called a *machete* that looks a lot a Hawaiian *ukulele*. Is it coincidence? Not in this case! In fact, in the late 1800s, Portuguese missionaries brought *machetes* to Hawaii. The instrument became so popular, it even got a Hawaiian name.

A number of American instruments have brother and sister instruments in Africa. Why? Certain instruments were carried between Africa and the United States between the 1500s and 1800s, when many Africans were captured and brought across the ocean as slaves.

Long-necked lute, Cameroon

Irish *bodhran* The *bodhran* is a frame drum that is hit with a stick called a *tippen*. It is believed to have been brought to Ireland from Asia by Viking explorers nearly a thousand years ago.

Banjo, United States
The American banjo is a reinvented form of an African long-necked lute. Can you see the family resemblance?

Spanish guitar being introduced in Peru, 1600s

Hammered dulcimer, Hungary This instrument has strings that are struck with a small mallet, so it operates and sounds a lot like a piano without the keys. The only difference is that the hammered dulcimer is small and lightweight enough to be strapped onto a person's back. Indeed, the instrument has done a lot of traveling! It originally came from Persia, and as a part of gypsy culture, wandered around North Africa, Spain, and Central Europe.

Ukulele, **Hawaii** The Portugese folk guitar, or *machete*, is small enough to travel easily. When Portuguese missionaries brought it to Hawaii in the late 1800s, the Hawaiians liked it so much, they adopted it for themselves! They called it a *ukulele*. This Hawaiian name comes from the nimble way the musician's fingers jump about the strings, almost like little crickets. *"Uku"* means "insects," and *"lele"* means "jumping."

Though the Africans could not bring instruments on board the slave ships, they were able to bring them in their memories, creating similar instruments using American materials. The banjo, in particular, has specific African roots.

Staying Tuned to Tradition

As time has passed and technology and trade have become more developed, some kinds of musical instruments have taken a leap into the future. These days, you can find computers capable of producing entire symphonies in full stereo sound. Electronic music has revolutionized the way many people study, play, and record music.

But at the same time, traditional musical instruments have far from disappeared! In fact, many cultures make a special point of keeping the art of playing their traditional instruments alive. Is there a musical instrument that's a part of your culture or family heritage?

Musical instruments can provide a window to the world outside your own culture. In some instances, they reveal the differences between cultures—

Hardangerfele, Norway
The *hardangerfele* is a folk fiddle decorated with beautiful Norwegian folk art.

Huti, a folk fiddle of the Pashtun people of Afghanistan

Moog synthesizer A synthesizer creates music by producing electric sound signals. Synthesizers can make all sorts of unusual sounds. They can even imitate other instruments!

Spike fiddle, Mongolia Spike fiddles, which have long necks and are held vertically, are common in Asia, Africa, and the Middle East.

Tarahumara Indian fiddler, Mexico The fiddle is a stringed instrument that is played with a bow. One of the world's most common folk instruments, the fiddle is found in various shapes and sizes all over the globe.

how our customs, climates, musical tastes, and histories vary. Other times, the way we look at musical instruments shows us just how similar we are to people all around the globe.

Tuareg woman playing an *anzad* (one-stringed fiddle), Niger

Glossary

accompany to occur with (p.21)

ancestor a relative who lived in the past (p.18)

appropriate suitable; proper for the situation (p.16)

culture the beliefs and customs of a group of people that are passed from one generation to the next (p.4)

deduce figure out (p.14)

elaborate having much detail (p.22)

environment a person's natural surroundings (p.12)

gender whether someone is male or female (p.22)

heritage a tradition handed down from the past (p.30)

melody the succession of musical tones that makes up the leading part in a musical piece (p.5)

missionary a person sent to convert other people to his or her religion (p.29)

orchestral used in or with an orchestra (p.7)

professional skilled enough in some activity to make that activity one's occupation (p.4)

repentance regret; remorse (p.21)

revolutionize to make a complete or extreme change in (p.30)

rhythm the repetition of a beat or sound, usually in a regular way (p.9)

sacred deserving of honor or respect; holy (p.18)

sacrifice something given up (p.21)

samurai a Japanese warrior (p.27)

significance importance (p.6)

symbolize stand for (p.20)

technology the scientific methods and ideas used in industry and trade (p.30)

tradition something that is handed down from generation to generation (p.4)

vibrate to move back and forth rapidly; quiver (p.10)

Index

Afghanistan, 30
Africa, 4, 6, 8, 13, 14, 18, 20, 26, 28
Apache people, 14
Australia, 15
Austria, 16
bagpipes, 10, 13
banjos, 28
bells, 4, 16, 26, 27
Bolivia, 6, 7, 12
Borneo, 18
bull-roarers, 18
Cameroon, 13, 28
Canada, 19
castanets, 17
China, 20
Colombia, 22
conch shells, 8, 19
Czech Republic, 13
Denmark, 15
drums, 12, 13, 15, 18, 19, 20, 21, 22, 26, 27, 28
Egypt, 13
electronic music, 30
England, 11
Ethiopia, 20, 21
Fiji, 9
flutes, 5, 6, 7, 16, 22, 23
France, 11
Germany, 26
Ghana, 10, 16, 22
gongs, 5, 18, 26
Great Britain, 24
griots, 4, 25
Guatemala, 14
guitars, 10, 12, 20, 28, 29
harmonicas, 24
harps, 23
harpsichord, 11
Hawaii, 28, 29
horns, 5, 11, 26
Hungary, 19

India, 5, 19, 22, 23
Indonesia 5, 9, 14
Inuit people, 19
Ireland, 23, 28
Japan, 5, 16, 23, 27
jaw harp, 16
Kenya, 7
keyboard instruments, 11
Mexico, 6, 10, 31
Mongolia, 10, 31
Morocco, 20
musical bow, 8
Niger, 4, 31
Nigeria, 27
Norway, 30
Papua New Guinea, 12, 18
percussion instruments, 5, 10, 11
Peru, 21, 29
pianos, 22
Polynesia, 6
Portugal, 28
rattles, 9, 15, 19, 20, 21
Russia, 16
Scotland, 10
scrapers, 8, 9
Senegal, 25
Siberia, 18
Spain, 17
string instruments, 5, 9, 10, 11, 13
Switzerland, 17, 24, 25
Tahiti, 8
Tibet, 21
Trinidad, 15
trumpets, 10, 14, 20, 21
United States, 4, 8, 26
whistles, 4, 26, 27
wind instruments, 10, 11
xylophones, 5, 14
Zaire, 25
Zimbabwe, 19
Zuni people, 9

About the Author

Sara Corbett is a writer who lives in New Mexico. This book is dedicated to her father, who plays the bugle, the slide trombone, the ukulele, the guitar, and even has his own player piano. He has taught her how much fun musical instruments can be.